A ROOKIE READER

PURPLE IS PART OF A RAINBOW

By Carolyn Kowalczyk

Illustrations by Gene Sharp

Prepared under the direction of Robert Hillerich, Ph.D.

CHILDRENS PRESS ®

CHICAGO

Library of Congress Cataloging in Publication Data

Kowalczyk, Carolyn.
  Purple is part of a rainbow.

  (A Rookie Reader)
  Summary: Introduces vocabulary and the concept of
parts of a whole with examples such as a petal on a
flower and a whisker on a kitty.
  1. Readers (Primary) [1. Vocabulary] I. Title. II. Series.
PE1119.K77   1985   428.6   85-11693
ISBN 0-516-02068-4

A petal is part of a flower.

A raindrop is part of a shower.

A feather is part of a bird.

A letter is part of a word.

A finger is part of a hand.

A drummer is part of a band.

A smile is part of a clown.

13

A jewel is part of a crown.

A tire is part of a truck.

A bill is part of a duck.

A building is part of a city.

A whisker is part of a kitty.

A sail is part of a boat.

A beard is part of a goat.

A window is part of a house.

A tail is part of a mouse.

A child is part of a family.

28

And a family is part of this
big, big, big, big WORLD!

WORD LIST

a	feather	purple
band	finger	rainbow
beard	flower	raindrop
big	goat	sail
bill	hand	shower
bird	house	smile
boat	is	tail
building	jewel	tire
child	kitty	this
city	letter	truck
clown	mouse	whisker
drummer	of	window
duck	part	word
family	petal	world

About the Author

Carolyn Kowalczyk loves writing and children. She has a degree in Psychology from the University of Oregon and is inspired to write by her experiences in foreign countries. She studied in France, taught English in Japan, and is presently in Germany writing and working as a nanny. Through books we learn about the world, and when we learn more about the world we see how very much the same people are. Especially children!

About the Artist

Gene Sharp has illustrated several books in the Rookie Reader series including *Too Many Balloons* and *Please, Wind?* He would like to dedicate the pictures in this book to Laura who loves pictures and Alan who is learning to also love the words.